YOUR KNOWLEDGE HAS VALUE

Anonym

The Construction Of Meaning In "Black Dogs" By Ian McEwan

GRIN Publishing

Imprint:

Copyright © 2008 GRIN Verlag GmbH
Print and binding: Books on Demand GmbH, Norderstedt Germany
ISBN: 978-3-656-87189-7

This book at GRIN:

http://www.grin.com/en/e-book/286727/the-construction-of-meaning-in-black-dogs-by-ian-mcewan

GRIN - Your knowledge has value

Since its foundation in 1998, GRIN has specialized in publishing academic texts by students, college teachers and other academics as e-book and printed book. The website www.grin.com is an ideal platform for presenting term papers, final papers, scientific essays, dissertations and specialist books.

Visit us on the internet:

http://www.grin.com/

http://www.facebook.com/grincom

http://www.twitter.com/grin_com

Black Dogs

by

Ian McEwan

The Construction of Meaning

Introduction

Statements, texts and events deliver information and construct meaning. We create meaning every time we speak. The construction of meaning is affected by various parameters, for example to a certain degree by personality. It therefore is seldom, if ever, an objective matter. Events can be interpreted differently and hence mean different things to people. The interpretation of events is, for example, based on the readers' as well as the novel's characters' experiences and philosophies. Also, the way a novel is composed, i.e. the way it is written as well as its style and wording, has an impact on its interpretation and therefore on the construction of meaning.

In the novel Black Dogs, written by Ian McEwan, June and Bernard have different philosophies of life. Bernard is rational and strongly believes in science and its logic whereas June is rather intuitive, spiritual and has a metaphysical understanding of the world. Part of my work will be to show the impact of different philosophies of life on the interpretation of events, which again causes different meaning. June and Bernard represent diametrically opposed views of the construction and interpretation of meaning. Also, June's and Bernard's attitudes and personal experiences affect the construction of meaning.

Furthermore, various textual connections between events and incidents play an important role in the interpretation of the text.

On the basis of the ideas outlined above I will interpret particular passages, identify and analyse the construction of meaning and outline their significance.

Characters' ideologies affect the creation of meaning

On June's and Bernard's honeymoon trip to France June undergoes an inner struggle. She moves from her current notion of life – her passion for Communism and the countryside – towards developing a new meaning of life, a metaphysical understanding of the world. The turning point is the encounter with two black dogs. Two black dogs do not inherently mean anything; they are simply two black dogs. However, a certain meaning is constructed around the encounter and the black dogs in general.

The two black dogs are described as being of "unnatural size" (144) and appearing as "mystical beasts" (144) "bred for aggression" (145). These 'creatures', as June calls them, slowly, but steadily move towards June and are insinuated of "having a plan" (149), which means they act reasonably. This is a clear formation of a symbol: for June the two black dogs stand for 'evil' and pose a risk. The way the black dogs and the whole the incident are described create a certain atmosphere and construct a very clear meaning. Besides, June is separated from Bernard who, as her husband, should protect and defend her against all dangers. The reader shall be convinced to accept the meaning of June's encounter with the two black dogs as created upon the incident by June: these two black dogs are not some usual dogs, but they represent evil. But, primarily, June constructs meaning of the situation for herself. She analyses the incident in a very particular way and draws her personal conclusion from the encounter.

Meaning is created by the choice of words and by building up the tension of whether these two "evil creatures" kill June. A person with a different belief and, for example, a more rational attitude towards life might have described an encounter with the two black dogs differently and hence would have created a different meaning.

Bernard's scientific approach towards life stands in total contrast to June's:

> *"Laboratory work teaches you better than anything how easy it is to bend a result to fit a theory. It isn't even a matter of dishonesty. It's in our nature – our desires permeate our perceptions."* (89)

And this is exactly Bernard's view towards June's 'story' of how she has experienced the turning point of her life. June constructs the meaning of the events in that very particular way it suits her best to justify her new spiritual, mystical attitude towards life. Bernard as her human guardian and whom she has called and looked for while facing the two black dogs has not saved her. So, *"she tried to find the space within her for the presence of God"* (149) and to her, there is no point of discussion that God or some other greater power has responded to her cry for help and has given her the strength and determination to resist evil.

Her construction of meaning justifies her change in life, i.e. the adoption of a mystical word view.

Also, the 'Dragonfly Incident' (see passage p. 75 – p. 79) deals with the protagonists contrary philosophies of life. Bernard follows the principle of rationalism and a scientific approach of reasoning whereas June is non-rational and spiritual. On their honeymoon trip to France, Bernard catches a dragonfly. He has June hold it in order to get out the killing bottle and take it home.

To Bernard, the entomologist, the dragonfly is a "beauty". Dragonflies are genetically clones and hence have no individual rights. His logic as a scientist is that this should be reason enough for him to kill, store and inspect it. June defines the dragonfly as a living being that has the right to live. June, currently being pregnant, stands in for the 'idea of life', not only aiming on protecting the foetus inside her but all living subjects around her as well. Also, she fears consequences if she is not able to protect life, for example the dragonfly's life.

Bernard's reasoning is somewhat illogical; however, he manages to make June's statement appear illogical in the way the event is told. Meaning is constructed by telling the event in a certain way. The truth is not in the event, but much more in telling the event. Bernard imposes his will and constructs meaning in the way that it fits what he believes is the truth

June's 'idea of life' and especially her mystical fear of nature's revenge are strengthened by Jenny being born with a sixth finger. In European arts a dragonfly traditionally symbolizes evil, in contrast to the butterfly which generally stands for goodness. Even though this 'evil' creature is killed nature takes revenge. Jenny being born with a sixth finger proves June's correctness regarding the 'idea of life' and especially her spiritualism and mysticism.

Bernard and June both construct different meaning around the 'dragonfly incident', based on their philosophies.

The reader's knowledge affects the creation of meaning

During Bernard's and Jeremy's visit to Berlin as the Berlin Wall falls Bernard gets involved into a street fight. Bernard intervenes as a young Turk is attacked by a group of young, bold-headed men, of which some have swastikas pinned to their lapels. The whole situation (see passage p. 95 – p. 100) can be interpreted in various ways and different meaning is created depending on the level of background knowledge the characters involved as well as the reader have.

Reading only this particular passage as an excerpt of some unknown book a very different meaning of Bernard's action to intervene would be created than looking at this very same passage in context to Bernard's life, i.e. embedded in the complete the novel. Without any background or contextual knowledge the reader would repeat Jeremy's question *"Did he really think he was too old, too tall and thin, too eminent to be hit"* (p. 97) too himself / herself and might take this incidents as some evidence for Bernard being somewhat insane or naïve.

However, background knowledge indicates that there is some deeper meaning. The Nazis' physical and behavioural appearance is described in a way that the reader inevitably recalls the black dogs, representing 'the evil' in June's encounter with them and being the reason for a core turning point in June's life. Being aware what black dogs stand for it becomes clear that this intervention must be a significant and decisive moment in Bernard's life as well. By intervening Bernard wants to achieve more than simply preventing the young Turk to be beaten up by some Nazis. Much more, Bernard is presented with an opportunity to enter the practical world and redeem himself. The connection to the black dogs shows how important this opportunity is to Bernard.

So, without knowing about Bernard's past and the black dogs it is barely possible to recognize Bernard's purpose of intervening. Meaning is constructed differently depending on the background knowledge of the reader, i.e. the knowledge about Bernard's past enables the reader to interpret the situation deeper and to make sense of the situation. Meaning is created by linking current actions to past events and experiences.

Character's past affect the creation of meaning

Similar to Bernard's intervention in Berlin Jeremy cannot resist from intervening in an incident of violence. Jeremy, similarly to Bernard, is driven by his past to take action and protect the weaker party in an act of violence. The connection of current events to past personal experiences creates meaning and emphasises events.

During a trip to France, Jeremy stays at the Hôtel de Tilleuls. One night during dinner in the hotel restaurant a young boy is violated by his father. The mother takes no action to intervene and to protect the child.

Jeremy calls this incident an "embodiment (...) of my preoccupations" (126). The young boy is about seven years of age. Jeremy is struck by the boy's loneliness while being at the restaurant with his parents. The boy is about the same age Jeremy was when his parents passed away. After his parents have died Jeremy has suffered severely from loneliness. Due to this fact Jeremy feels some kind of connection between this boy and himself and himself during his own childhood. There is a second aspect that makes this situation intolerable to Jeremy. His niece Sally has experienced violence at home by her parents Jean and Harper. Jeremy feels guilty for not having intervened and protected Sally. On the basis of these connections between Jeremy's past and what the boy faces this passage gains importance.

Similarly to Bernard's reason for getting involved in the fight in Berlin also Jeremy attempts to make up for what he believes has caused guilt over him: he has not protected his niece Sally from her parents Jean and Harper (see p. 16 – p. 17). Jeremy describes beating-up the young boy's father using the same sort of words he uses for describing the fight in Berlin (compare p. 98 and p. 131). However, after Jeremy lets off from the boy's father he does not feel proud or relieved. Much more, he is "horrified with myself" (131). Based on Jeremy's feelings one can derive from this passage that violence should be answered with even stronger violence. Before engaging in the fight, Jeremy says to himself that someone needs to intervene, but not himself. Generally this is a 'wrong' attitude. However, instead of fighting with the father Jeremy should have attempted to reach a non-aggressive solution. This is exactly what Jeremy notices after the fight. He recognizes that that anger, traumatic personal experiences and personal connection to the victim do not justify violence.

So, meaning is constructed by implicitly making a statement against violence in general, in this case the father against the boy and Jeremy against the father. The passage seduces the reader to believe it is tolerable, desirable and correct to beat-up the father, i.e. being violent. The reader is demonstrated how easy it is to get in a position in which one supports the person that takes steps of violence, i.e. Jeremy against the boy's father. The reader of the passage becomes emotionally involved on the basis of what happens to the child and especially by recognizing the connection between Jeremy and the child. This is the trigger to make violence appear an appropriate way of solving conflicts. After the fight, Jeremy recognizes that he has lost control and the evil of his deed. Jeremy's enlightenment (131, "horrified with myself") is an implicit lesson and warning to the reader not to act violent not to tolerate, support or allow violence to happen.

Conclusion

Facts and reality have the meaning what we apprehend of it. The characters and readers of a novel can have very different associations with certain incidents, people or animals, for example with the black dogs. To June, for instance, the two black dogs stand for something evil whereas to Jeremy they rather cause happiness. To Jeremy the black dogs have a rather positive meaning. Partly, this is probably the case because the black dogs and June's encounter with them have fascinated and attracted Jeremy from the very first moment eventually have made Jeremy a part of the Tremaines.

The text shows that meaning is, in general, a matter of perspectives. A character's or reader's perspective influences the construction of meaning around incidents, people and all kinds of events. As outlined in the main body of the essay a novel's character as well as a reader's perspective is determined by philosophies, experiences and knowledge.

The 'dragonfly incident' shows the different approaches of logic and reasoning, based on June's and Bernard's diametrically opposed philosophies, towards the 'idea of life' or the value of an insect's life. The significance of (background) knowledge, to both a novel's character and a reader, is demonstrated in Bernard's intervention in a street fight. Jeremy's intervention in the restaurant of the Hôtel Tilleuls shows the impact of personal past experiences on the meaning and value put on specific events. Also, to the reader the style of the text strongly impacts on his or her creation of meaning. As analysed above, the description of the black dogs, especially the choice of words, leads the reader towards following and accepting June's view of the event, as the black dogs are described – June tells the story out of her perspective – solely with words that carry a negative connotation.

Bibliography

McEwan, Ian. 1998. *Black Dogs*. London: Vintage Books.